INTRODUCTION

The ability to sight-read fluently is a most important part of your training as a violinist, whether you intend to play professionally, or simply for enjoyment. Yet the *study* of sight-reading is often badly neglected by young players and is frequently regarded as no more than a rather unpleasant side-line. If you become a *good* sight-reader you will be able to learn pieces more quickly, and play in ensembles and orchestras with confidence and assurance. Also, in grade examinations, good performance in the sight-reading test will result in useful extra marks!

Using the workbook

The purpose of this workbook is to incorporate sight-reading regularly into your practice and lessons, and to help you prepare for the sight-reading test in grade examinations. It offers you a progressive series of enjoyable and stimulating stages in which, with careful work, you should show considerable improvement from week to week.

Each stage consists of two parts: firstly, exercises which you should prepare in advance, along with a short piece with questions; and secondly, an unprepared test, to be found at the end of the book.

Your teacher will mark your work according to accuracy. Each stage carries a maximum of 50 marks and your work will be assessed as follows:

> 2 marks for each of the six questions relating to the prepared piece (total 12).
> 18 marks for the prepared piece itself.
> 20 marks for the unprepared test. (Teachers should devise a similar series of questions for the unprepared test, and take the answers into account when allocating a final mark.)

Space is given at the end of each stage for you to keep a running total of your marks as you progress. If you are scoring 40 or more each time you are doing well!

At the top of the first page in each stage you will see one or two new features to be introduced. There are then four different types of exercise:

1 **Rhythmic exercises** It is very important that you should be able to feel and maintain a steady beat. These exercises will help develop this ability. There are at least four ways of doing these exercises: clap or tap the lower line (the beat) while singing the upper line to 'la'; tap the lower line with your foot and clap the upper line; on a table or flat surface, tap the lower line with one hand and the upper line with the other; 'play' the lower line on a metronome and clap or tap the upper line.

2 **Melodic exercises** Fluent sight-reading depends on recognising melodic shapes at first glance. These shapes are often related to scales and arpeggios. Before you begin, always notice the *key-signature* and the notes affected by it, then work out the finger patterns on the finger board.

3 **A prepared piece with questions** You should prepare carefully both the piece and the questions, which are to help you think about and understand the piece before you play it. Put your answers in the spaces provided.

4 **An unprepared piece** Finally, your teacher will give you an *unprepared* test to be read at *sight*. Make sure you have read the *Sight-reading Checklist* on page 17 before you begin each piece.

Remember to count throughout each piece and to keep going at a steady and even tempo. Always try to look ahead, at least to the next note or beat.

NAME		

EXAMINATION RECORD

Grade	Date	Mark

TEACHER'S NAME	
TELEPHONE	

STAGE 1

More patterns in $\frac{6}{8}$

RHYTHMIC EXERCISES

MELODIC EXERCISES

PREPARED PIECE

Marks*

1 Explain the time-signature. How many beats will you count in each bar?

6 quavers per bar - 1 23 4 56, 1 23. 456

2 What is the key?

C minor

3 Clap the rhythm:

4 What is the letter name of the first note in bar 13? *Ab*

5 What do the following mean: *rall. (rallentando)*? *slowing down*
   cresc. (crescendo)? *getting louder*
   dim. (diminuendo)? *getting quieter*

6 What does *Andante sostenuto* mean? *moderately sustained*

Total:

Andante sostenuto

p   *cresc.*   *f*

dim.   *p*   *cresc.*

f   *rall.*   *dim.*

Unprepared tests page 18

Mark:

Prepared work total:

Unprepared:

Total:

*The mark boxes are to be filled in by your teacher (see Introduction).

STAGE 2

F♯ minor

RHYTHMIC EXERCISES

MELODIC EXERCISES

PREPARED PIECE

1 What does *Allegro con moto* mean?   Walking speed with motion

2 What is the mood of this piece?   Sad + lyrical

3 In which key is the piece written?   F# minor

4 Where might you add a *poco rall.*?   bar 8

5 What will you count?   2 beats in a bar

6 Which bar will be the loudest?   bar 11.

Total: ☐

Allegro con moto

Unprepared tests page 19

Mark: ☐

Prepared work total: ☐

Unprepared: ☐

Total: ☐

Running totals:

1	2

STAGE 3

The triplet

RHYTHMIC EXERCISES

MELODIC EXERCISES

PREPARED PIECE

1 What is the key of this piece?

2 Clap the rhythm:

3 What does *pp (pianissimo)* indicate?

4 Will you begin with an up or down bow?

5 What does *Andante con moto* mean?

6 Whar does the sign 𝅗𝅥 indicate?

Total:

Andante con moto

Unprepared tests page 20

Mark:

Prepared work total:

Unprepared:

Total:

Running totals:

1	2	3

STAGE 4

More complex rhythms in $\frac{6}{8}$

RHYTHMIC EXERCISES

1

2

3

MELODIC EXERCISES

1

2

3

4

PREPARED PIECE

1 In which key is this piece written?

2 What does *Poco lento* mean?

3 Where is the climax of this piece?

4 What will you count?

5 What is the character of this piece?

6 What does *meno mosso* mean?

Total:

Unprepared tests page 21

Mark:

Prepared work total:

Unprepared:

Total:

Running totals:

1	2	3	4

STAGE 5

F minor

RHYTHMIC EXERCISES

1

2

3

MELODIC EXERCISES

1

2

3

PREPARED PIECE

1 In which key is this piece written?

2 What does *Con moto* mean?

3 What will you count?

4 How much bow will you use for each of the three opening notes?

5 What does *leggiero* mean?

6 How will this affect your performance?

Total:

Unprepared tests page 22

Mark:

Prepared work total:

Unprepared:

Total:

Running totals:

1	2	3	4	5

STAGE 6

More complex ties

RHYTHMIC EXERCISES

1

2

3

MELODIC EXERCISES

1

2

3

PREPARED PIECE

1 In which key is this piece written?

2 What are the main technical demands of this piece?

3 Which two bars contain syncopated rhythms?

4 How will you interpret *p dolce*?

5 What is the implication of *molto moderato*?

6 What preparation will you have to make for the final note?

Total:

Unprepared tests page 23

Mark:

Prepared work total:

Unprepared:

Total:

Running totals:

1	2	3	4	5	6

STAGE 7

RHYTHMIC EXERCISES

MELODIC EXERCISES

PREPARED PIECE

1 In which key is this piece written?

2 What does *Scherzando* mean?

3 What does *sonore* mean?

4 What does *meno mosso* mean?

5 What key is the meno mosso section in?

6 What does *accel.* mean?

Total:

Scherzando

meno mosso

mf sonore

accel.

cresc.

a tempo

poco rall.

Unprepared tests page 24

Mark:

Prepared work total:

Unprepared:

Total:

Running totals:

1	2	3	4	5	6	7

CONCLUSION

A sight-reading checklist

Before you begin to play a piece at sight, always remember to consider the following:

1   Look at the key-signature.

2   Look at the time-signature, and decide how you will count the piece.

3   Notice any accidentals that may occur.

4   Notice scale and arpeggio patterns.

5   Notice dynamic and other markings.

6   Look at the tempo mark and decide what speed to play.

7   Count one bar before you begin, to establish the speed.

When performing your sight-reading piece, always remember to:

1   CONTINUE TO COUNT THROUGHOUT THE PIECE.

2   Keep going at a steady and even tempo.

3   Ignore mistakes.

4   Check the key-signature at the beginning of each new line.

5   Look ahead – at least to the next beat or note.

6   Play *musically*.

18

UNPREPARED TESTS
STAGE 1

STAGE 2

STAGE 3

STAGE 4

1   Larghetto

2   Allegro ma non troppo

3   Vigoroso

STAGE 5

STAGE 6

STAGE 7

1   Andante cantabile

2   Lento

3   Con moto